The Smell of Purple

Dónall Dempsey

The Smell of Purple

© Dónall Dempsey

Fourth edition 2020

ISBN: 978-1-913329-07-5

VOLE Books

15 Rosetrees
Guildford
Surrey
GU1 2HS
UK
01483 571164
dempseyandwindle.com

A catalogue record for this book is available from the British Library

For Shyam
because of his great love
for his daughters
Sonali & Khushi

Contents

Foreword

One of Dónall Dempsey's great intuitive strengths as a poet is his empathy with the people of his childhood, but most specifically his empathy with the child he once was. Some of his strongest poems work as they do because they nail down the immediacy of the universal experience of being young and innocent. But in all those poems he also fully realises the minds and perspectives of the adults around him: his mother, his father, uncles and aunts. Imbued with life, they step out of the poetry and into the mind's eye of the reader, until the reader is blind with the seeing of the poet.

These intuitive strengths are at the forefront of Dempsey's latest collection, The Smell of Purple. This entire book is the author's journey through fatherhood, but a fatherhood that becomes an extraordinary selfhood as child. Once again we become blind with the seeing of the poet, journey with him through the wonders of fatherhood, become mentors of the child of the poems, marvel at the purity and vivid imagining of the child's mind; become, essentially, children ourselves in the perfectly-visioned childhood perspective of this delightful collection.

John W. Sexton
Poet, author, lyricist and editor

BECOMING TILLY

You saunter by
curled up in your mother's belly

carried regally from place to place
your little kicks a Morse Code

we are unable to decipher.

EASTENDERS sending you to sleep.
Mozart 40 quickening the beats.

Mummy's tummy goes before her.

Each day the dragon grows
her tattoo twisting into

the Cyclops of her navel.

One day her belly button
pops out

as if you had upped periscope
to see what seas awaited you.

Meanwhile you sail on
to ... through ... towards

this particular day
the day of your berth,

unafraid as yet
of Fridays & 13th's

dropping anchor at 7 of the clock
this early morning

the longitude & latitude
of your charted time.

Your mother smiles.

Her cries and your crying
giving birth to such

happiness
you

(who you are & who
...becoming.)

TEA FOR THE TILLERMAN
sings the room as blindly you

search for the tiller to steer yourself
through all your days

tacking into life
narrowly avoiding the reefs of Death.

Your name only then
bestowed upon your life.

'Tilly!' we call you
'Tilly!' we call to you

and you unseeing
yet wise

set course
for your times

giving us
a right royal wave.

Be brave
little girl

sail into
the future that awaits you

guided by the star
that is

your name.

AND THE SUN ALWAYS SHINES MAGENTA

I live in a crayonned house that opens onto
a multicoloured view of whatever

has taken her fancy.

A little purple tree with a large orange apple
wave after wave of the bluest grass.

My little girl, larger than me, holding my tiny hand
both of us taller than house or tree.

A rainbow of smoke undulating from a fat chimney.
A dog barks across a white sky

('I got tired & couldn't
be bothered to colour it in!' she explains)

Big blue birds flying around our feet.
This crayoned house lives on a wall

of a bedroom you haven't lived in
since you were small & drew us here

with stuck out tongue & intensity of hand.
Now drawn by Time we return

(good old Dad & dutifully grown daughter)
step into our crayoned world

as if it were yes(only yesterday).

ME! HOW?

all her dolls
in brand new bright blue frocks
her cat too

THE SOUND OF THE SOUND

All day she mooches about the house
mouthing invisible words

(a little human goldfish.)

'Tilly ... just what are you doing?'

'Shhhh ... I'm listening
to the sound of the sound

... when it doesn't come out!'

MATCHING MICKEY MOUSE PLASTERS

Polly dolly grins
as I sew her up
stops bleeding sawdust

daughter and dolly
both wearing
matching Mickey Mouse plasters

LITTLE MONKEY

The potted plant
looks startled

its Mediterranean blue ceramic
lies here ... lies there.

It looks
for all the world

as if it has just grown
out of the kitchen titles.

'Tilly?'

my voice interrogates her
with just a question mark.

She squats on her hunkers
looking as startled as the flower

covering her eyes
with her palms.

'Till...y?'
the question mark

probes deeper
into her fear.

She puts her fingers in her ears
her baby blues still shut tight.

'T...illy?'

the question mark rounds her up
like a sheep dog would.

She clasps her palms
over her gasping pout.

She whimpers.

I laugh & cuddle her up,

my three wise monkeys
all rolled up into one.

POEM PLANTING

Words flow in different coloured thoughts
from your tiny hand

page after page submits to your mind
crayoned into being.

Then we tear them up into separate entities
plant them in the rich black soil

between row after row of crocus.

Planting words
you squeal with delight.

I tell you they will grow into poems
by the morning if ... you love them enough.

As you sleep
(dreaming that it can be – such)

I kidnap your words
shape them so that when you awaken

a tiny crop of haiku
awaits your happily believing eyes.

We read them
over soldiers and perfectly boiled eggs.

SWING LOW SWEET CHERUB

I watch your behind
perfectly perched

upon the swing
fly over the breakfast things.

'You're flying too high!'
my voice nervously warns.

You pay no attention
and kick the 'yooow!' cat.

You swing nakedly, a little cherub
lost in a world of your own.

'She's not a little cherub ... she's a little nuisance!'
Mum scolds her.

'Why did you have to make her a swing
indoors for God's sake!'

Mum scolds Daddy.

Daddy and Tilly
smile.

FIRST PERSON SINGULAR

Everywhere I look
all things gather

into their respective
collective nouns

suddenly the air is alive
with an *ascension* of larks

such an *exultation*!

whilst here
upon this ground

an *ostentation* of peacocks
preen & spread

their awesome fans
Granddames at an opera.

Their shrieks shatter
the peace of the park.

A *scurry* of squirrels
scamper through trees.

A boy squirrel chases a girl squirrel
up their favourite tree.

I follow them

watch as they merge
in a blur of foliage.

A *swarm* of bees are doing it.

Birds, it would appear
are everywhere doing it.

Here a *clamour* of rooks
there an *unkindness* of ravens!

What next, I laugh to myself

a *parliament* of owls ... an *implausibility* of
gnus

A *skein* of geese stretch like sadness
across a sky becoming sunset

and leave the world
to darkness and to me.

TWO LITTLE GHOSTS

Two little ghosts
shuffle down the street

looking very frightened.

A gang of skeletons
break out into a clatter of laughter.

A girl ghoul & a boy ghoul
hold hands

dressed in their best
mouldy school uniforms.

A moon laughs
at a bunch of little devils

who should know better
… but don't.

Witches are a bit more scarcer
on the ground this year

than last Halloween

thinks the real ghost, amused at the humans
dressing up in their greatest fear.

BEING ADAM IN THE GARDEN OF EDEN

I tell my little girl
the collective names

for what we see
moving about the farm

she delighting
in the newness of the sounds

the unbelievability
of the obscure:

here a peep of chickens
there a clutch of chicks

moving swiftly along
to a murder of crows

mesmerized by a mischief of mice
chuckling at a clutter of cats

tickled by a kindle of kittens.

The language keeps
blossoming into terms

unknown by her
until then.

'Do it again!' she pleads 'Do it again!'

'A scurry of squirrels...a lamentation of swans!'

She squeals with delight.

Even one of her goldfish
changes its name to Charm.

They used to be
Bewitched … Bothered … & Bewildered.

But I can't tell which one is Bothered now.

Next day we journey back in sound
substituting the unknown

part of the collective noun
for the thing itself.

The farm transformed

into kindles and clutters ... clutches & peeps
scurries & lamentations ... mischiefs & murders.

So that even in the future
a single kitten will become her kindle.

At night she sprinkles the tiniest of food
upon the meniscus of her goldfish bowl.

'I'm feeding them stardust!' she maintains

charmed by her charm of goldfish
a solitary cat her clutter

(people think she's speaking a different language
and in a way she is.)

'I love naming!' she giggles.
'It's like being Adam in the Garden of Eden!'

THEM BONES!

'So, my skeleton
is alive inside me?'

She asks (apropos of nothing)
as we breakfast.

Her bowl Snaps, Crackles & Pops!
as she awaits my confirmation of her

deduction.
'Well … yes … I guess!'

I answer her

I smile at her
milk moustache

and a single Rice Crispie
clinging to her curls.

'It's just like my shadow
but inside me holding me up!'

she extrapolates to her rag doll.

Her dolly doesn't comment
as if she were (like me)

thinking it over in her mind.

She slurps her juice too fast
so that she splutters & laughs.

Then she jumps
off my knee

and dashes off
breakfast slopped across the table top.

'Tilly … where you … going … Tilly?'

'I'm taking my skeleton for a walk!'

AND ONE…AND TWO…AND. . .

she's teaching the cat
to waltz
the cat ain't taking to it

THE ONLY WAY OF LOOKING AT A BIRD
(for Glyn Pope)

she looked at the bird
with all of her self

as if by some alchemy
of thought

she flew into its shape

as it became the air,
her mind opening

its wings
to the sky

the house now a little blue egg
far far below her

her voice curving
into a beak

that flung its being

into the song of self
scrawled across a sky

becoming sunset
so that

becoming human
again

was a grief
that could only be

expressed
in birdsong.

MANY CHILDREN AGO

An old broken doll
remembers her first Christmas
many children ago.

Now, only the rain
plays with her hair.

MANY REMEMBERS AGO

Tilly tells me tales of herself
from the so long ago

(down to the incrediblest littlest detail.)

I'm amazed she can do so.

'How can you remember that?'
I ask ... shocked.

'Oh, I remember many remembers
they just walk into my head

& tell the story all over again.

I just listen & tell what the story telled me
even if it is many many remembers ago!'

Years later when she has grown
so far away from here

her hand fallen from mine

a Goth Punk Princess,
now only men on her mind,

she doesn't remember any of the remembers
remembered then.

But I remember them for her,
she too busy remembering the Future

& the kisses it will bring.

TELLING TILLY TALES

Almost as if I hypnotize you
you gaze entranced

as the words flower from my mouth
your tiny hands trying to grasp their

blossoming
crying 'cos you can't

catch them and now
with anguished anger

trying to tear them from my lips
the treasure of speech

as if it's a magic trick you can't quite figure out,
this mystery of words

you want to hold in your hands
that you can only hear in your heart

this ghost of breath
that dies with its birth

the wonder of words
that blazes behind your eyes

setting your mind
on fire.

TILLY IN WONDERLAND

Slowly … she studies the mirror.

Slowly... she studies
(herself) in the mirror.

Suddenly she darts behind the mirror
amazed to find the image of her

'... gone! '

Cries to herself she's lost herself.

Next day I superglue two mirrors together
so that now she exists … whichever side she is!

She calls herself 'Me! '
on this side

& 'Me! Me! '
on the other.

Her mother wonders why Tilly
(my little Alice)

only answers now to the name
'Me! Me!'

She explains to her cat
this new-found fact of her two-ness.

He seems happy with that

accepts whatever she says.
He becomes 'Cat! Cat!'

At bedtime she cleverly insists
that Tilly stays up & that 'Me! Me!'

'… goes to bed …'cos she's tired
but Tilly's not!'

In the morning
'Tilly no want go school! '

'Me! Me! go!'
She stupid … can't talk!
School learn her talk!'

We have the suspicion
Tilly is smarter than

the two of us put together

& is adept at
utilising her doppelganger...

sending it to do the things Tilly
doesn't want to do.

We envy her
her belief

wish we could do that too!

MR. DADDY SOFT SOFT

Always her fascination with me
shaving.

This her early morning ritual
observing each action

as if it were holy.

I hide my face in foam.

'Santa Claus! Santa Claus!'
she chants,

winces with delight as the razor
(she gulps)

goes over my bump without
(gasp) slicing it off.

The shaving uncovers the *me* she knows.

'Soft … soft … Mr. Daddy Soft Soft!'
she gurgles in a lather of laughter.

'Me now … now me!' she pleads with me.

I take the brush … coat her reflection with foam.
I shave her … with the tip of my little finger.

Her reflection sniggers & she sniggers too.

Later, in the early evening
she appears

bearded in fresh cream.

She shaves herself with a lollipop stick.
'Me ... Daddy now ... see!'

I cha-cha-cha her on the tips of my toes
as she clings to my fingertips.

The living room dances around us

one delighted half shaved little girl,

one delighted soft soft Mr. Daddy.

NEWBORN

I love the lullaby of you.

Your voice cuddles me.
Your laughter swoops like a swift

little bird alighting upon my attention.

Your name comforts me.

Your words drip like a honey
I can almost taste.

Your smile caresses me.

My name trickling across your tongue
explodes like fireworks

from brain cell to brain cell.

Your beauty catches my breath
as if you blew gently across my face.

I am lost in a sea of you
caught up & swept away

by *everythinganything* you do.

I only a new born father
just getting used to

the wonder of you being my little girl.

DÓNALL SAID ME

Your 3-year-old search for words
trying to grasp them as I speak them

seeing what you are hearing
as a tangible thing

sound a something you can touch
me deceiving you

to try to please you
with the truth of lies

confusing the issue with my trickery
me stupidly

tearing a scrap of paper
scrawling, 'Tilly! Tilly! Tilly'! on it

placing it secretly
like a holy wafer upon my tongue

like a little bird calling 'Tilly! Tilly! Tilly'
& you

peeling your slippery name
from my voice

wild & wet with amazement
running with wonder to Mummy

with a 'Look ... look ... Dónall said me!'

the mystery of your world
curling up at the edges

held in the palm of your hand.

GIRL SQUIRREL

I wait for your awakening.
And yes, there are things I could be (should be) doing.

But.

Now I find I can't do anything without you

and your constant interrupting of my known world
with the simple fact of yourself.

I wait for you to wake so you can exist me,
bring me into being.

You stumble
towards me as if sleep were a net

that still entangled you.

Placing yourself against my shoulder
you name me to make me real.

I heave you up
against my head

the little heft of you
the perfect weight of you

like a dream that has come true

dribbling my name down the back
of my open necked shirt.

I attempt to dress you in the necessary
clothes that constitute a walk in the park

but to you clothes are playthings.

You wear your pink teddy bear knickers
on your head, big bunches of hair

sticking out where the legs should be
as you wee-wee over my hand.

'Oh naughty wee wee!'
you chastise yourself.

I take an age, amazed at what
a Mummy can do in a minute or two.

Finally, with only your eyes showing
I strap in my little Ninja

& we go
visit the trees & squirrels & swings.

You want to know if it is a girl squirrel.
I can't tell but tell you that it is.

A bird sits on the swing
beside the swing you swing upon.

You accept it not as a bird
but as a fellow-traveller

learning the ways of this alien world
& how to control a Daddy

so he does exactly what you
wish him to do.

THE TELLER OF TALES

Fragile as a little bird you alight on my lap
weighing no more than a dream or a wonder would.

You adjust your bony bum,
perch & command me to begin:

'Say... the story!'

This is how the story always begins
eyelash to eyelash, chin to chin.

You gaze into my eyes as if the story already
exists there and my voice just colours it in.

Whether it be Grimm or Hans Christian Andersen
you never take your eyes off my eyes.

Your little hands hold the sides of my face
so (you say) you can feel: 'The way the words move!'

And night after night
to your and my ever greater delight

You say: 'Say ... the story!'

And the night listens as the big human

weaves a world for the little human
(to get lost in &) find herself again.

Precious as water, little daughter,
I carry your sleeping & put your dreams to bed.

WEATHER FORECAST

my little girl
looks me in the eye
'I think this is the weather for sweets!'

THAT'S...ONE SMALL STEP...

Vest on
(inside)(out)

2 legs in one
knicker hole.

shoes on (back to
front).

'I dressed my
self by my
slef!'

'Mmmm...so I see!'

'So I see!'

MY LITTLE NUMERO UNO

She attacks the page
with all the fervour & ferocity

of learning to write:
! nUmBeRs!

Her pen digs its way
through to (the other page)

as if it were trying to escape its task,
make a break for it.

Finally, she draws
a 2

a gentle swan
gliding by on a single wave.

Then, an 8
(which she informs me)

is an O
'...wearing a belt that's too tight.'

'Right? '
'Right! '

6 & 9
she cuddles together.

'Shhh...they're sleeping! '

Then: a 3 ... which is
'an 8 with half the 8 ... missing.'

Then: a 1 which is a man
'… with a little nose.'

Then: a 7
which: '… is a man with a big nose.'

10 is:
'The man with the little nose
going out with an eight without its belt.'

5 is:
'Like a S frozen stiff.'

4 is:
'My hand doesn't like writing 4's so ... I doesn't!'

'Well, that's enough of that!'

She glares at me as if to say:
'Don't dare contradict me!'

'And now…I'm going out to play!'
she proudly announces

(a woman with her work well done) .

And out...out she goes!

THE FOREVER FLOWER

She hands me a stalk.
'The flower's dress
fell off!'

'Fix it!' she cries.
I by sleight of hand
fix her flower but with a different colour.

'It's a different colour!'
'The flower...' I tell her
'. . .changed its dress!'

This flower
with its dress fallen off
I hold forever.

HEADING FOR A HORIZON

'The grass is crying!'

So Tilly sees it & so...it is...so.

The dew glistens (the grass listens)
both laughing at her passing fancy.

Soon the sun wipes away all its tears.

The grass chuckling (being chased back &
forth)
by a south westerly breeze

that Spring has sprung upon us.

Tilly crying with delight

her kite hungry for the open skies
head-butting the clouds, snapping at the wind

making her dig her little feet in
fiercely as if (any moment now)

she could take off (losing a sandal)

she clinging on for dear life
like crazy to her crazy kite

mad now with height

I clinging on to her fly-away ankles
the landscape becoming a patchwork quilt

chatting to a passing bird

heading for a horizon.

MAKESHIFT DADDY

She wraps her legs around my neck
pulls on the reins of my ears and curls

when she wants me
to giddy up or stop.

She screams: 'Daddy Daddy!'

and excitedly wee-wees down
the back of my neck,

A happy little girl
happy that I am her Daddy

... even just for now.
'You're my pretend Daddy

'cos my real Daddy's gone away
to be dead in Heaven.'

She tells me that one day
she will visit him in Heaven

but she will '... have to wait
until she's grown up dead.'

'But...'
(she carefully assesses the situation)

'...you'll do
for the time being!'

AS ABOVE SO BELOW

I show her the stars.

'Are they ours?' she whispers.
'Only if we name them!' I answer

as the Universe undresses itself before us.

I name the stars for her
making up names for the stars I don't know
... the names of.

'This one is yours...it's a Tilly star!'

I show her how to hold it
between forefinger& thumb

gently gently
I tell her what constellations are.

Next night the moon finds her

arranging her collections
of pebbles shells & stones

(taken from the mouth of rivers
taken from the sides of seas)

adopting a star's position
mimicking each constellation.

'I want to be able to see them
even when I can't see them!'

All that sunny Sunday
her constellation of shell & stone

shone brightly
in the noon day sun.

FEELINGS

her kitten dies
'My feelings are leaking
out of my eyes!'

ETERNITY IN A GRAIN OF SAND

She takes an old broken cracked conch shell
a dried-up Corsican starfish

sand from her backyard sandpit
(slightly damp)

dumps them all on her nice clean new sheets.

'I'm bringing the seaside to bed!'
she announces

her creation
(like a little God.)

Hours later I peep in

to find her
asleep by her seaside

dreaming it ... for real.

I tuck her & her seaside up
gently

against the coming cold

tiptoe away

trying not wake
either.

GATHERING WATER

Never having encountered one before
except in stories

my daughter begging to be taken to the well
the source of all her fascination

a magical tale in itself
letting the bucket fall into the nothingness

that soft splash as if from a different universe
& she a charmed girl

the well eating her pebbles eagerly
greedily as if it were hungry for her wonder

the delayed ... plop ... enthralling her
and again ... and ... again

even when our store of water
miraculously grows

and we have more water
than we can shake a stick at

she orders (or commands rather)
'Come...father, let us go & gather water!'

And I (ha ha 'Father!' is it now)
get up & go gather water with my little daughter

enchanted by the fairytale of her laughter.

6 O'CLOCK SHOCK!

Our sleeping naked bodies
nothing but mere landscape

hills & dales of flesh
to be tramped across

by the tiny patter of your little feet
as they trample us –

we both come awake in sudden shock.

'Want a cuddle!'
you announce in your imperious tones

& despite our obvious pain
we acquiesce at once, drag you in

slaves to your love
wrap our warmth & our flesh about you

And soon all three of us snoring now as if we
were The Three Bears of the story I had read to you

sleepily
the night before.

CUDDLES

She climbs upon my knee
& then wobbles
almost topples ... off!

I catch her & HO! HO! HO! her.
Ask her what does she '... want

for Christmas
little girl?'

Suitably Santa'd

she plants a foot
on each of my patellas

stands firm like a miniature
Colossus of Rhodes

holds on to my neck ... kisses me.
'Me want cuddles!'

A tear trickles down my cheek.
She laughs & licks it off.

We cuddle.

BECOMING THE RAIN'S LANGUAGE
(for Shyam)

the rain
writing upon the lake
in its own strange script

I dive
hide under its waters
watching the rain writing

gasp now for breath
I emerge back into this world
rain writing upon my face

the rain writes
in Urdu
I its living page

*I was asked... why Urdu... but... why not. I didn't
know at first the rain's script (I thought it was the
rain's own language) but gradually became aware
that it was indeed Urdu... naw... I go to Delhi in
January and was reading some ghazals by Mir and
Ghalib. And so... Urdu! Also the poem was a gift
for my friend Drifty (a poet can only offer a gift of
words) so I thought let's have the rain write in
Urdu.*

We were swimming in a beautiful clear lake ...
swimming through the reflections of trees standing
on their heads ... swimming through clouds ... when
suddenly the rain started writing upon its surface. I
could see the writing happen ... half Morse Code ...
half unknown script ... I sank below its waters to
discover the rain falling in this underwater
dimension ... I saw it write itself from another
world ... when I broke back into the world of air I
gasped with surprise as the rain wrote upon my
face and I became its page.

STORYTIME

in the flicker of shadows
she tells them stories
her dolls sit on the stair and stare

AUNTIE COMES TO TOWN

she was long
in a wide way
3 seats across

when she laughed
all of her laughed
an earthquake of flesh

she had a chin
underneath her chin
and then another chin

when she hugged you
her breasts surrounded you
took you prisoner

once she stumbled
tumbled on to the cat
we had to get another cat

the cat
was like a horror movie
only realer

was always afraid
she would tumble onto me
I didn't want to be a real horror movie

the cat said nothing
all his lives
squashed flat

I liked Auntie Mabel but
she had whiskey kisses
spat when she spoke

always glad when she's gone
I feel I have somehow survived
an act of God

MORE TEA?

'Auntie Mabel's voice...'
(she sotto voce's me loudly)
'...smells like a fart!'

'Hush!' I try to shush her
'But she does...she does!'
'Her voice is farts!'

wish I could sink into ground
'More tea...Mabel?' I smile
offering her another jam tart

THE SMELL OF PURPLE

She says she can smell yellow.

She says she can smell blue.

despite not being able to
spell either colour.

'Yellow smells the same as blue

... like a wet kitty drying by the fire.

Red smells like
Mummy when she kisses.

Her kisses smell different
when she kisses you ...

... then she smells like flames
with little orange tips!

Purple is my favourite smell...
... it smells just like a magic spell!'

I kiss her goodnight
like lilac (only lighter)

with little flecks of purple
scattered here & there.

BABBY DADDY

in your tiny hand
I become a crayoned man
much better than I am

Blu-tacked to the fridge
I an icon
made holy by my child

'I love my b a bb y!'
you name me in rainbow
all my 'd's' look the other way

tongue almost bitten
in two with concentration
'I'm writing a painting!'

*The sort of moment that a father tucks away in his
own emotional wallet and takes out every now and
then. She was my teacher and told me how to look
at the world in her own brightly coloured way.*

*Oh, she was so adorable ... so she was! She then
came up with 'I'm painting a writing!' So they
were twined somehow inside her head and fused
together with her little knowledge of the world. But
she spoke truer than she knew! When it came to
doing her name in Chinese letters with a brush
then you could see how right she was!*

LES DOLLS

she complains to her dolls
about me
'SAYS TO ME...NO MORE SWEETS!'

the dolls
gasp at such cruelty
'Tut! Tut' they pout 'Tut! Tut!'

'Bastard!'
screams her rag doll
God, she's got a mouth on her!'

she mocks my voice
'SAYS...NO MORE SWEETS!'
'What..!' I say. 'Nothing!' she says

moans to her dolls
they are all on her side
look at me with disdain

the dolls lie around
trying to trip me up
laugh silently when they do

NOW I LAY ME DOWN TO SLEEP

She sobs her heart out
'My ... im ... imag ... inary friend
won't talk to me!'

'So, everyone has to die?'
'Even ... my dolly!'
she goes away and cries.

Her teddy watches over her
till she falls asleep
then ... falls asleep itself.

The teddy
clings to its child
scared of that Jack-in-the-Box

TAMED IN BLUE BUCKETS

She brings me
the sea to see
in her tiny hands.

Tamed in blue buckets
the captured sea
sleeps beside her bed.

I la-la-la her,
she claps & dances
'I like when you music me!'

the sea laps
the hem of her skirt
like an immense tame monster

*It was my little girl's first meeting with a sea
... she looked so tiny and fragile ... the sea
looked like a monster that came and bowed
at her feet. I noticed every little molecule of
her ... alas I didn't write back then so I have
to go back to the past and recreate her atom
by atom. You ever tried to drag back (atom
by atom) a very reluctant sea? It's like trying
to take a Kraken for a walk on a leash.*

OG

'... og!'
You command the language & it…obeys you.

Providing you with a dog.

A sleepy dog who when he hears you
wakes up trundles over to you

slumps at your feet & then goes back to sleep.
You…the Queen of Words.

'Ahhhh... og!' you stroke the word
& it obeys your every whim.

'Dog!' I say.

He opens an eye &...looks away
as if to say: 'Who's him... then?'

Ahhhh ... my little cave girl I love
your little explorings of the tongue

and how the world comes when it is bidden.

'Dada!' you pronounce
& I too come at once

tied to the invisible string of your voice.

CUDDLE

'Awww... come here!'
she said to the ghost

giving it a cuddle.

It hadn't been cuddled
for a long long time.

It began
crying.

*I brought my little 'daughter' to see her real Daddy.
It was the first time she had ever been in a
graveyard. She looked at an angel crying marble
tears amongst the rain but didn't cry herself. She
looked at a point in mid-air as if he were there and
comforted him wherever he was.*

'Daddy's not dead ... he's alive in my head!'

I began crying.

COW COUNTING

She counts cows
'... a cow... another cow &
another another cow!'

It doesn't all add up
as yet
but she's got the gist.

'How many cows... ?'
'Millions!'
she's discovered hyperbole.

The four cows
enjoy being 'millions'
'Moo!' they moo over her 'Moo!'

'They can only say Moo?'
'They are still only...' I tell her
learning to talk!'

'Moo!' she tells the cows
'That means goodbye
in their language!'

Another cow appears
'How many cows now?'
'That many fingers!'

EN LAKECH!
(I AM ANOTHER YOURSELF)

(for Jo Van Bargen)

Attempts to (smuggle Snuggles)
into her bed,
one very little girl pregnant with cat.

'Eh...ex-cuse me young lady & just where
do you think you are going with that cat?'
'CATS IS PEOPLES TOO!' she sniffles.

She's...got me...there
'CATS IS PEOPLES TOO!'
her little logic slays me.

Cat & girl
all legs & paws akimbo
dreaming the same dream.

GIRL TALK

Her cat cradled in her lap
her frock a hammock

she talks to her cat
& the cat talks back.

They both purr with the pleasure
of each other.

'What do you talk about?'
I ask, curious to know.

'Oh ...you know ... cat things!'

I leave them at it.

BEING TILLY

'Tilly!'
'Get down before you … !'

Like a kitten
she tiptoes across the piano's keys

her footsteps leaving a trail of discordant notes
all F sharps & E flats

before she falls in a crashing crescendo
from major to minor

of notes sprawled across the softly carpeted floor.

'Tilly! Tilly!' my voice tries to catch her in mid-fall
now she lies sulky all legs a-kim-bo.

'I felled my self!' she announces to her self

disgusted that she failed in her scales.
'Tilly. . .I told you don't play on the piano!'

I scold her now that the fear has gone.

'Me ... not Tilly today!'

'Oh & ... just who are you?' – 'Me ... Frank!'
'Frank?' – Yes ... like Teddy!'

(Frank is her terrible tatty teddy)

'When I grow up I want to be a teddy!'
'Oh ... you do, do you?'

Tomorrow she will be Tamara
& then the day after Tamara ... a little Lulu.

Doesn't accept a name is a thing to be tied down to.
She changes it day by day

a different name being a scapegoat for
the nightly naughty things she does

when sleep & counting sheep doesn't seem to work.

And today she's yes ... Scheherazade
She soaks up stories like the process of osmosis.

Scheherazade fails to last
the obligatory 1000 & one nights ... but nearly does.

There's a tinkle from the moon-cast next room.
'Tilly!'

'You on that piano again?'
(she never figures out how I know.)

'No ... Lulu is!'
'Naughty Lulu!' she scolds her other self.

'Tilllllllllllllllllllllllllllllllllllly!'

MUMMY DYES HER EYES

'Mummy dyes her eyes!'

'Mummy dyes her eyes?'

'Yes!'

'She is blue today & green yesterday!'

Mummy's different coloured
contact lenses lie

upon her dressing room table
beside her Pond's cream

and various other unguents.

She chooses ... changes her eyes
to match her clothes

Yes...Mummy dyes her eyes.

SEEING STARS

High noon. The roads ... melt.

Too hot for barefoot: 'Ouch, ouch and ouch!'

Your footsteps trapped in tar ... the sun is God.

'Ra ... Ra ... Ra!' she intones in unknown Egyptian
as if she had stepped from a millennia or two ago.

She walks hand in hand with her rag doll.
'Dolly' gets dragged everywhere she goes.

She stands before me as if she were a President-to-be
about to make a speech.

'The stars. . .have come on in my head!'

I fear an injury and that what she's seeing
are stars like in cartoon land.

'Nooo....not like Foghorn Leghorn or Pepe le Phew
(her favourite two.)

'The stars in my mind running around my memory!'

She walks off with constellations (blooming inside her)
dragging an ever-patient Dolly by the hand

THE GHOSTS OF VOICES

'I like the way
the music swims towards me
through the air!'

my little one
afraid of records
'... 'cos of the ghosts of the voices...'

the ghosts of voices
trapped
forever in shellac

ORDINARY MIRACLE

she watches the treasure
of an ice cube
melt through her tiny fingers

'Again...again!' she implores
this her
ordinary miracle

PRETTY AS A PICTURE

she brings me the tape recorder
'Quick... take
a picture of my voice!'

THE SWEETNESS OF NOTHINGS

She whispers in my ear.
('. . .whisperwhisperwhisper. . .')

'What...what I can't hear?'

'That's because I've put a secret in my voice!'
she whispers.

'If you could hear it … it wouldn't be a secret!'

'Tell it me again!'
I beseech.

('. . . whisperwhisperwhisper . . .')
go the wordless words.

'Ahh...I see!'
I say

hearing

nothing.

FAVOURITE PHOTO

'I like this photo of me!'
She cradled it happily in her palm.

The photo was old and looked sleepy.
I could see it dreaming itself.

'You're in it too!'
I looked & couldn't see me anywhere.

Your head had been cut off and most of your eyes
(only the lower lashes showed.)

Golden curls grew on your shoulders like epaulettes.
You wore a lovely smile and nothing much else.

I squinted: 'But where am I?'

'That hand is you!' she smiled her lovely smile.

A hand all alone had crept spider-like
just in to the left-hand bottom side of the photo.

'Tilly took it when she was two!'

FAIRY TALES CAN COME …

My little daughter wants to be Cinderella
& go to the ball with Mummy & Daddy

& so we banish the babysitter (so wickedly pretty)
(who still gets paid just to be banished.)

Dress our darling daughter as if she were a fairy story come
true … a spangled tutu ... wand ... and ballet shoes.

I sweep up my little pumpkin
and carry her like a male fairy godmother

to the ball of balloons and cocktail laughter
and dance with my little streamer-strewn princess.

But even a princess can tire of excess
ends up asleep under top hat ... opera scarf ... and coat.

Later I carry my sweetness through street after street
careful not to wake or spill her dreams

... remembering to steal her left hand shoe
... waking her just as midnight bongs
so that she knew...

But now she sleeps (and sleeps believing)
that fairy tales can come true and that

... they can happen to you with a Daddy who tweaks
reality... just that little bit ... just for you.

BEING LITTLE

Granny plays along
will be my little girl's 'little girl'
even eats up all her greens

Granny quite enjoys
being a little girl again
& having a little girl for a 'mummy'

'Now... who's ... the mummy here!'
my little girl scolds my granny
Granny smiles and goes to bed meekly.

Soon, too soon
the responsibility of being mummy grows
heavy
she falls asleep as her own little little self.

Early morning
both 'girl-girl' & 'Granny-girl'
still snoring

I tiptoe from them
wishing I could be the boy I was
but dawn breaks open a new day

IN THE LION'S MOUTH

You stand in the lion's mouth

like an X come alive from an alphabet
or a chromosome.

Your feet stand firmly on its roaring tongue.
You tread it down as your hands uplift

the frightful jaws...the ferocious teeth.

You smile and look very sweet.
A perfect little girl happy with herself.

You made this lion photo-frame yourself
(and so are not afraid of it.)

You shaped and fired it,
its gaudy colours delighted with themselves.

And now you stand here real as a photograph
placed between such teeth,

hold time at bay
a little girl in the big lion's mouth.

I FEEL PRETTY... OH SO ... PRETTY!

I
...a...
   ...wake

covered in glorious glitter
smelling strongly of PVA glue

sticking to my cheek
very

hung-
-over

& covered in blueorangeyellowred feathers

a bubble recently blown
perched upon my nose

I ... still ... half coma ... tose

tiny bubbles travel amongst my curls
as through a bigger bubble brightly

nestling neatly over my right eye
I observe my tiny daughter

purse her lips & kiss
more bubbles into being.

  'Till...y!' I force my lips

(still frozen in sleep)

to somehow speak:
'What...you...do? '

(Even my syntax and sentence structuring is shot.)

She smiles sweetly: 'I'm
...pretty-ing you! '

OLD DOG, NEW TRICKS

'The dog's in the loo!
We was teaching him to pee
and he just fell in ...'

SLEEPING WITH TWIGS

My little daughter strikes
two stones together
'They're talking..!' she informs me.

little daughter
to her this stone
a wonder of the world

sticks...twigs
become precious
to her touch

she sleeps with a twig
found that day
loyal to its personhood

all things alive
in her eyes
loved with equal delight

WORD BAGS

Here on Saturday she tells me
'My Sunday words
can't wait to be said!'

'All my Saturday words
are almost wasted!'
she lapses into silence.

'My word bag for Saturday
is almost empty but
my Sunday words are filling up!'

'Your Saturday words are almost all gone?'
I ask in adult disbelief.
She nods a silent yes

'And you've got a bag full
of Sunday words filling up!'
Yet again she nods a 'yes.'

At this astounding news
I discover my word bag
is almost empty too.

Both of us speechless now
waiting for Sunday's words
to turn up.

THE SMELL OF THE LIGHT

Tilly tells me
she 'adores' the smell of the light.

Watches intensely as I fiddle with the wick
of our battered kerosene lamp.

I smile as her eyes light up.
Love how she loves everything with a passion.

'Adore' is her new-found-much-used-word.

So now she *'adores'* the rich ritual
of lighting the lamp and all its accordant magic.

Hand in hand we scatter the darkness
that snarls & reluctantly backs away

but then creeps back behind us
its tongue lapping at us

licking its lips as if it would swallow us up
but it is afraid of the smelly light.

The wind tries to blow us out.

Scared, she clutches me all the tighter.

'I don't like the way the light
makes the darkness darker.'

Her voice shivers.

I catch her up in the crook of my arm.
She cuddles closer as we walk on towards the barn

adrift in a sea of darkness,

we the only speck of light (no stars tonight)
we the light of the world,

the pregnant cow lowing
as if it knows we are coming.

Tilly nuzzles into me, a frightened little mouse
jumping when an owl demands of us: 'Who..who..who!'

'Your chest is too tickly!' she complains sleepily.

'Ah... yes. My little chickadee!' I W.C. Fields her.

This never fails to amuse her,

our intertwined laughter & the smell of the light
dispelling the darkness,

the pregnant cow delighted to see us.

THE NOT DARK

'I don't like the dark!'
she whispers into my hair
'I prefer the not-dark!'

CONVERSATION BETWEEN
A PUDDLE AND YELLOW WELLIES

the puddle winked
and in a sunlight voice
'Oh go on...jump! Jump!'

her yellow wellies
answered with delight
'Plash...splash...plash!'

I IS SMILING

Everything always is:
'I is...'

As in:
'I is ... happy!' ... 'is ... tired! '

Even to negate it, is:
'I is ... not tired!' 'I is ... not go bed!'

(with Churchillian scowl
& foot stamp for emphasis.)

I used to love your construction,
the simple syntax of your sentences:

'Tilly & Mummy ... is girl!'
'Dónall Dónall is ... not girl?'

Now I is
remembering you

just as you was

recall your words just as they is

& I
I ... is smiling.

SMACK

she smacks the road
hard...sobs
'Naughty road for falling me!'

FIRST FISHES

.•´‾`•.,,><((((°>
in and out
,.•´‾`•.,,><((((°>...°°°
among her thoughts
,.•´‾`•.,,><((((°>...°°°
her first-seen-fish still swim
.•´‾`•.,,><((((°>

LISTENING

little daughter
puts her fingers in her ears
'I'm listening to my thoughts!'

A STEW OF DÉJÀ VU!

A rolling ball
of knickers & curls

knickers & curls
that un-curls…un-coils

flies backward
through the sky

to stop in mid-air
in a starburst jump

as she returns to balance
precariously on top of Rover's house

Rover too trotting backward
into his kennel

his silent barks backing off into silence

then it all happens
over&overagainover&over ... again

as she (the mistress of
the rewind button)

controls her tiny film self
laughing with glee

'Look at me…look at me!'

NATURE V NURTURE

'Blahblahblahblahdeblah!'
she spits the sock

out of her mouth.

'What on earth Tilly
... are you doin'?'

'You told me to put a sock in it!'
she grins.

Oh now…she's inherited
my sense of humour

and my penchant for a sight gag.

Her mother pontificates:

'It's your own fault ... I think
it's more nurture than nature!'

'None of our family would do stuff like that!'

Tilly & I just laugh
& like how we are.

MY LITTLE SAPLING!

A strand of light blonde hair
gently blown back & forth

across your amazed face
by your own breath

held now in wonderment

as you watch
in the tiny compact world of the pot

the first little green hair
sprout tentatively from the black earth

remembering the time
we two planted it

not knowing the when or how
it would grow into oh...

... such wonder.

Turning your baby blues up at me
barely capable of speaking the words

your mouth full of awe
you explaining it back to me:

'It growed ... oh ... it growed! '

STICKS

She clutches her 'sticks'
two twisted twigs she's just picked up

but which to her are precious.

All her other toys just loll around
forgotten now as the dinosaur

gazing out the window where she had placed
him
to look at clouds & clap her hands & laugh.

A rag doll throws herself across a chair
weeps & tries to remember

the touch of her hand
the smile that never ceased to surprise her.

She prods herself with her twigs
chortles with glee as the twig sinks in

& the flesh gives way
leaving little designs upon her.

It amuses her the way the skin
reasserts itself & becomes her again

whether it be thigh or belly or knee.

'Me drawing on me with sticks!'
she announces proudly.

After investigating her own skin
she investigates mine & Mummy's

delighted with our
exaggerated 'Ows!' & 'Ouches!'

that she 'draws' out of us.

'Oh ... ouches!' she smiles fascinated
that it also elicits sounds.

And now our little explorer
falls (still clutching)

asleep
(her sticks)

these her
most precious objects.

She our
most precious object.

FOOTSTEPS SET IN TIME

The lightness of your footstep
as you hurried to me

caught in the slowly setting concrete
(you didn't see)

holds your fleeting love permanently
your footsteps greedy for me

paying no attention
to the world whatever

only knowing that
in a few footsteps more

you would be precious
and adored for who you are.

Your footsteps still exist
echoing inside my tears

as I put my next step (inside yours)

and the snow fills
the other footsteps up

WRITTEN ON THE WIND

I teach her her letters
anywhere we go, take it off the page.

The heel of a boot dragged through snow
becomes the S she now knows,

a fingertip across a frosted window pane
is a capital T

with trees and a winter sky showing through

or a bathroom mirror fogged over
forms letters from its mist.

A small c & a capital C is tickled upon her belly.

Two crossed forefingers ... an X
a Y is drawn invisibly upon the air

We get used to writing on the wind
drawing letters then full and fuller sentences

so that we have long conversations
writing on the space between us

gesticulating, madly in love with the words
that own us

in love with the words that form us
in love with the words that love us.

IF PARADISE IS HALF AS NICE

Yawns into my morning wearing only my
Edvard Munch's THE SCREAM Tee-shirt

which is a mere miniskirt on her
scratching a well-tanned behind.

All smeared mascara ... all Cleopatra eyes
all mad crazy hair ... mad as a bag of spiders

dancing (sleepily to) Amen Corner on the summer radio.

Takes my toast from my poised hand takes a bite crunchily
puts it back in exactly the same position.

Pats me on my head: 'Mmmmmm... thanks Dad! '

'Stolen toast is always twice as nice!'
Sings softly, swaying, to herself,

'If Paradise is half as nice as the Heaven that you take me to
...(Ooops ... slops spills her orange juice)
'... who needs Paradise ... I'd rather ... have you! '

Then suddenly excitedly talking to boyfriend No.22
on her little pink glitzy mobile.
Guess my little girl ... has (gulp) grown up!

USING UP ALL HER THOUGHTS

'You're very quiet?'
'Shhh... I'm letting my words
have a rest!'

'I'm breathing in
the dark so that
all my awake will be gone!'

'Ohhhhh noooooooooooooo
I've used up
all my thoughts!'

'I'm tired but
only my leg
has gone to sleep!'

all these years later
my little girl's words still
wander around my head.

MORE LASTING THAN FOREVER

ring you made
of sweet summer grass
more lasting than gold

you insert a daisy
into its green band
'That's its jewel!'

'I'll wear it forever!'
I tell her
and I do

even now
I wear the thought of your ring
more lasting than forever

your ring of green
invisible now
real as love.

Death calls me by my name.
I go unafraid,
your green ring upon my pinkie.

AN OCEAN SMILING WITH ALL ITS HORIZON

waves shyly lick
between her toes
as if she's tamed an ocean

an ocean
like a genie let out of a bottle
walking beside my daughter

an ocean
smiling with all
its horizon

some scattered birds
like thoughts
the ocean has thought up

not willing to leave it
she cries to the sea
'Shhhhhhh ...!' shushes the sea '... shhhhhhh!'

GOD BLESS DADDY

'… a prayer is a thought
you say
with all of your self…'

MAKING THE UNIVERSE

Together we created constellations
placed a star just ... here ... another there.

Formed Orion. Then ...The Great Bear.
Beteljuice flowed from our fingers.

You knelt in prayer
golden curls cascading over shoulders

you the perfect cherub.

'Our Father who art in Heaven...'

You prayed with all the might of being
just 3 & a bit.

10 packets later of day-glow stars
we had set the Universe to rights.

A FAIRY TALE OF RAIN

Running around in the rain
two little girls in the nip
'We're wetter than wet!'

Delighting in the rain
two little naked girls
squealing around a garden.

'It's 'orrible when clothes get wet!'
they yell in unison
'... but wet skin is the nicest thing!'

The rain & two
naked little girls
the best of friends

at one with the rain
their naked yells ...
their naked screams

'Bring 'em in!' Mum screams.
'Noooooooooooooo!'
'The rain's our friend!'

Teenagers now
they watch embarrassed
flickering images of them being small,

all so ago
upon a time
a fairy tale of rain.

BOX OF MEMORIES

The years cover them as much as this rich earth
her memories we dig up & there they are

good as new
all the things that used to be you

buried in a box.

Even the calligraphy survives the years:
'TILLY'S MEMORY BOX.'

Your teenage self takes your 3-year-old
left blue shoe … cradles it in your palm.

You have no memory of it, only us telling you
the story of the memory of *'it'*.

How the right blue shoe was irretrievably lost
on holiday, floated out to sea by a so curious you.

Somewhere before the horizon
sinking out of view.

But you wouldn't relinquish the left
(and what it meant.)

How you wouldn't go to sleep without it
clutched in your grasp for a year or more

until we buried it in this
box of 'Tilly things.'

A broken rattle
wrapped in silence

a chipped glass heart
wrapped in pink & blue tissue paper

a magnetic elephant clinging for dear life
to the bottom of the box

labelled 'TILLY'S MEMORIES.'

I watch you cry for you (and I cry too)
for your forgotten self,

big unreal tears plashing
into your open palm

as you retrieve from Time
the things that were yours.

Your frail body
sobbing against my shoulder

like you used to do
when you were my little girl,

a left blue shoe clutched in your hand
now & then

as you attend the resurrection of the you
you never knew until now.

HERE NOW I HOLD YOU

Here now I hold you
astonished at your newness.

One hand cups your bum
the other cradles your head

you poop into my palm.
You smile your smile … still unused to it and its magic

wave a tiny lazy hand as if you were Royal
& I an adoring subject.

The music of you plays in my mind as if I were
a mechanical piano…notes played by invisible hands.

Your skull has yet to get it together

the fontanelle pulsing as if each thought could be
seen beating like a bird against my hushed fingertips.

Years later (my hands so much older now)
I cradle your crying

stroke your Punk Goth hair as you weep
over your first 'real' boyfriend (he so obviously a jerk.)

Your constant wailing: 'Why... why didn't it work!'

My fingertips
caressing where thought once pulsed

your sweet secret self hidden from me now
in your growing up.

Afterword

Tilly totally enthralled and enchanted my world by making her world ... my world. She allowed me to share in the making of her world ... how she constructed it from the facts given to her ... she could take 2 and 2 and could come up with 5 or 7 or even 4 ... sometimes simultaneously.

She was fascinated with the world as it happened to her and I was fascinated with her fascination. She took the ordinary and made it extraordinary. She gave me the gift of her seeing and the world (long since jaded and faded in my eyes) became alive with the wonder of her seeing.

The poems are my belated attempt to thank her for how wonderful it was to observe her take the world in through her eyes and 'Tilly it!' She was my little wonder and I simply loved her.

The debate about the page or the voice ... I was with Tilly! I too wanted to touch the trembling beauty of a word and hold it in my palm like a quivering little bird.

Tilly was such a beautiful little girl and I was so proud she allowed me to be her makeshift Daddy. I wore the title like a badge of honour. Tilly was just pure delight ... a happiness made tangible and so beautifully ... real.

Dónall Dempsey

Dónall Dempsey was born in Ireland in 1956 and came to live and work in England in 1986. He had been a soldier, a builder, Ireland's first Poet in Residence in a secondary school, a bookseller and a poet. He liked being a poet best.

Tilly was Dónall's friend's little girl, left fatherless by his friend's death when she was a toddler. Dónall's role as 'Makeshift Daddy' began when Tilly started to explore and look for meaning in the world they shared. Understanding Tilly's view of the life of inanimate objects and her kitten, teaching her letters and numbers, and talking with her about her world, offered the poet Dónall revelations that he has never forgotten.

Long after Tilly and her mother had moved to another town and another life, Dónall collected from the corners of his mind the stories of his years of learning from Tilly and gave them form. Here he shows how she could make the ordinary extraordinary with poems that are full of marvels and full of love, as only a poet's account can be.

A review of *The Smell of Purple*.

'Dónall Dempsey has created in *The Smell of Purple* a poignant evocation of childhood, that moment when a child discovers for the first time the world with its beauty and pain. In *The Smell of Purple* Dónall lets the child give voice to these discoveries. He records how Tilly, the three-year-old of the poems, speaks in ways, with a range, that suggest nothing less than the source of the poetry. Dónall provides a framework, a context to help the reader receive her extraordinary expressions – true and absurd, insightful, elegant and passionate. *The Smell of Purple* becomes a dialogue between two poets –Tilly and Dónall – who together explore a place where delicate understanding and misconceptions can take place.

In his poem 'Tilly in Wonderland' Dónall draws in a third-party, Charles Dodgson (Lewis Carroll), to help adults follow Tilly's encounter with a mirror. Looking at her image in the glass she celebrates the wonder of seeing herself then turning the mirror she exclaims the image is 'gone', her self lost. Dónall glues a mirror to the dark side and Tilly calls the first image, 'Me' and the reverse 'Me Me'. And her cat becomes 'Cat Cat'. Her logic, as in Wonderland, is indisputable.

This book praises and grieves. It shows the frailty in an adult's bond with a child, the pain that separation brings; it reveals a child's strange bond with childhood itself that led Lewis Carroll's Alice to despair and a need to flee back to normality. 'A Cat in the Hat' – hats off to Dónall for bringing alive that prospect of childhood, reminding us of our need to respond in all seriousness with imagination, and with love, when a child gives his or her love.'

Paul A.W. Sutherland (poet, writer, editor and educator)

Acknowledgements

Thanks and appreciation are due to John Sexton for his support and encouragement of Dónall Dempsey's writing, and for providing the introduction to the first edition of this book when it was published in 2014, which we publish again in this edition.

Thanks also to Paul A. W. Sutherland, Michael Farry, Fiona Sinclair, Mandy Pannett, Brian Ings and other appreciative reviewers of Dónall Dempsey's books.

Many of these poems have appeared online and in print anthologies.

Other collections by Dónall Dempsey:

Sifting Shape into Sound (2013)

Being Dragged Across the Carpet by the Cat (2014)

Gerry Sweeney's Mammy (2017)

Crawling Out and Falling Up (2019)